DEBT *of* GRATITUDE

ANJALI KAKAR

authorHOUSE®

AuthorHouse™ UK
1663 Liberty Drive
Bloomington, IN 47403 USA
www.authorhouse.co.uk
Phone: UK TFN: 0800 0148641 (Toll Free inside the UK)
UK Local: 02036 956322 (+44 20 3695 6322 from outside the UK)

Published by AuthorHouse 07/13/2020

ISBN: 978-1-7283-5243-5 (sc)
ISBN: 978-1-7283-5244-2 (e)

Print information available on the last page.

Contents

Pixar 1
Apple 2
Google 4
Starbucks 7
Porsche 9
Harley-Davidson 11
Virgin 13
Tesla 15
Amazon 17
Emirates Airline 19
Maserati 21
Disney 23
BMW 25
Samsung 27
J. P. Morgan and Chase 28
Bank of America 30
Wells Fargo 32
Tuli Imperial Hotel 35
Jumerah Group 37
Twitter 38
Nike 41
Emirates NBD 43
Coke 45
Oracle 47
Microsoft 48
Toyota 51
Audi 53
Walmart 55
Boeing 57
Volkswagen 59
Citibank 61
PepsiCo 63
Facebook 65

Pixar

An unimaginable organization that creates a culture of passion among the employees.
Forging ahead unanimously is the concealed key.
Emerging with boundless innovation from Northern California.
This organization will indeed exceed and go beyond what one's limited mind can fathom.
Eleven blockbuster hits over the past fifteen years.
Drawing forth the highest potential without any fear.
Not constrained by intellectuality, driven towards commitment and passion.
The drive to succeed is drawn out of relentless choice, indeed not a fashion.
Ideas can surpass various boundaries, and Pixar is the flagbearer of the same belief.
Without inspired passionate leadership, results will miss creativity.
One single person with passion can illuminate the room that has been shrouded in darkness.
Employees must be linked and not ranked, a principle Pixar truly adheres to without submitting to mess.
Ideas stemming from team collaborations can do wonders.
A great idea handed to a mediocre team can create a reckless thunder.
Pixar concentrates on passionate leaders who can illuminate the highest potentials that lie within employees.
Hiring unconventional folks is truly gratifying.
Their principle to link is truly captivating.
Creativity must be an amalgamation of absolute dedication and fun.
Life should not be taken seriously, not holding people by the gun.
Endowed with innovative leaders and creating teams that are highly diversified,
Pixar has truly proven its legendary mark; it's been unconquerable for over a decade.
Pixar is truly an embodiment of diversity and creativity which cannot fade.

Apple

It believes in doing things differently.
It believes in challenging the status quo.
The way Apple challenges the status quo is by making its products beautifully designed, simple to use, and user friendly.
Apple just happens to make great computers.

This encapsulates Apple as an organization.
The invention of Apple is truly one of the greatest creations,
Owing immense amount of gratitude to Steve Jobs and the founders who inculcated innovation.
A strong belief to create products that would change the course of the world was the cause that Steve focused on.
Simplicity was the essence, focusing on being infinite; complexity deteriorated with time—done and dusted and completely gone.
Collaboration and cross-pollination allow Apple to bring forth the highest reservoir of potential that lies beneath.
Courage and honesty to admit when they are wrong keeps them grounded and on their feet.
Participation in markets where they can create something truly meaningful and contribute in a significant way is their primary goal.
Every employee is considered unique and imperative as he or she plays an individual role.
This deeply embedded belief is truly magnificent.
An existence to make great products, and that is relentless.
Creating simple and beautiful products that create immense value in the world.
Outlandish voices seldom appear to create a twirl.
A computer revolution that completely changed the course of human existence.
An organization that is completely dedicated to the cause without having any fences.
A core value to honour people who can change the world with their passion.

Consistency across the globe is inculcated in Apple's core values and not subject to fashion.
Creating immense value in the invention and creating something meaningful comes from a desire to bring change to this planet. Without a skip of heartbeat, Apple continues to forge ahead dauntlessly, intensively researched and fed.

Google

An astounding organization where everyone is treated with mutual respect.
Their employees deliver beyond what one can fathom; it is indeed inevitable to expect.
Google's unofficial motto, "Don't be evil," serves as a culture to empower employees to bring forth their highest potentials,
To organize all data and make it accessible to the world.
Google's search engine service creates a twirl.
Google is for the dreamers, learners, listeners, and the people who are paranoid, hard to please, easy-going, or scared.
Google is a place everyone aspires to be a part of.
Innovation and creativity are propagated within the organization.
The creator is without a skip of heartbeat and rewarded with appreciation.
Designing a beautiful user experience has been their primary goal.
Failure is an option, and the growth of all employees manifesting their innate potentials is their role.
All are encouraged to have a mission and a purpose; it opens the door to outstanding achievements.
Google focuses on the cause, paving the way to certainty without being dependent or causing a vent.
Allowing their employees to focus on the product, going beyond the comprehension of their minds is truly imperative.
What an incredible organization; its mere purpose is to truly give.
By believing in opening development to the world, Google is tapping into a huge community of all the top 1 per cent minds.
Running millions of servers worldwide,
Google acts as an instrument to one's greater growth without taking a ride.
Focus on people, their dreams and desires, and design and dare to innovate beyond what one can fathom.
Every millisecond counts; a human's happiness is crucial, becoming worthy of respect.

Illustrated above are some of the design principles; connecting heart to heart is a must.
Engaging people where they bring the world under one roof.
A courageous organization, indeed, that believes in engaging beginners, attracting experts, and being the benchmark of proof.

Starbucks

The mission that inspires and nurtures human spirits—
One person, one cup, and one neighbourhood at a time.
Starbucks acts with courage, challenging the status quo and finding new ways to grow.
Connecting with transparency, dignity, and respect,
The organization forges ahead tenaciously, without any tormented effect.
Performance driven through the lens of humanity.
A team that is built on an indomitable foundation, being courageous is the key.
Perpetuating this idea of making it your own.
Increasing its brand value, it has truly grown.
Connecting with humanity and being imperative to everything matters.
Established in 1971, this is an organization that refuses to hide growth or relentlessly shatter.
It surprises and delights people with its amazing flavours.
Life is indeed a series of choices; the wise rejoice, whereas the foolish reluctantly savour.
Embracing resistance with smiles on their faces is its core.
An undying spirit that creates curiosity among the customers wanting more.
Leaving a legendary mark is truly its embodied spirit.
Starbucks was destined to exist, without a heartbeat, not a misfit.
Turning ordinary into extraordinary is far beyond its vision, which cannot be comprehended.
Empowering their employees to create the experience of a lifetime continues.
Starbucks is holding its customers' expectations really high, paying its dues.
Encompassing people globally and serving them with a smile, thereby merging countries.
Under one umbrella, the aim of Starbucks withstands being swayed by some fancy feather.

Porsche

Founded by Ferdinand Porsche who, in the year 1931, incorporated a company under his own name,
Porsche is indeed the world's leading sports car.
Classic and stylish and dazzling with character, this car is a head-turner, glittering with a star.
Almost sixty-five years have passed, justifying the values that characterize its vehicles and work.
Ferdinand created a breathtaking phenomenon without a quirk.
A dream of a perfect sports car creates that spark in each of us.
Porsche surely surpasses distances, uniting people in harmony, laughter, and race.
The underlying principle is to always get the most out of everything without a trace.
To translate performance into speed and success is the main goal.
Ideas are the new language, carving a path for the new role.
More ideas per horsepower, this principle originates on the racetrack.
Embodied in every single one of these cars is intelligent performance.
Forging ahead with immense power and efficiency, innovation will always be its benchmark.
Porsche is the harmony of the design concept, design being the ark.
Form always follows function; it must prove itself along the way.
In the wind tunnel, on every mile of the road, shining with its morning ray,
Porsche is an expression of freedom, a unique attitude towards life.
It is the realization of a unique dream.
Porsche is the dream of millions, a ride that is cherry on the cream.
Anchored in society, it creates substantial value.
A legendary work that will always stand its ground, gravitating towards becoming better than yesterday, and serving its due.

Harley-Davidson

Harley-Davidson is an action-oriented organization.
Established in the year 1903, the company is known for manufacturing motorcycles.
It engages employees in desired behaviours that align with strategic business goals.
Telling the truth is Harley-Davidson's primary role.
Be accountable and operate with model integrity are its embedded values.
Valuing individuality and diversity is the cue.
Bringing forth the highest potential and inspiring others is solely ingrained.
Harley-Davidson is progressing towards fulfilling its mission.
Adversity is the springboard for success,
Overcoming obstacles that act as instruments to the company's growth.
Creating an experience that creates value through their motorcycle products,
Harley-Davidson will continue to be one of the best brands across the globe.
Over a decade of leadership has expanded its value with its rewarding robe.
It is indeed a classic organization.
Ideas can surpass hindrances, and so is Harley-Davidson's expansion.

Virgin

An extraordinary leadership and the employees are the backbone.
The rules are palpable and not written in stone.
Richard Branson is a phenomenal leader who puts his employees' interests first.
Inspired by passion, Virgin Atlantic hires those who have the thirst.
It is a company that is focused on growth and adaptability.
Sir Richard Branson has the ability to think differently and an eye for talent, and created a positive company culture to listen, with a hands-on approach to learning.
A truly commendable leader who is acting as a coach.
Virgin Atlantic Airways, with its head office in the United Kingdom, is truly well known.
Its transformational leadership truly deserves a crown.
An entrepreneur, adventurer, activist, and business icon are what Richard Branson highlights for everyone.
Listening, learning, and laughing, along with empathy, are his principles and fundamental core.
The main goal of Virgin is to provide a seamless experience.
Indeed, it's the vision of Branson's creation,
Resulting in positive impacts on its customers, people, communities, and environment,
Creating thousands of jobs across the globe.
It is magnificent and inspiring and deserves to be on the red robe.
Its leadership style fits the organization and optimizes the talent available.
Leadership is a choice and not a forced decision.
People having the drive and a good cultural fit for the business are imperative.
Successes happen from working and learning with some of the most inspiring and inspired people.
Dwelling on setbacks will lead nowhere; focus on the upcoming goal.
Leadership is truly Branson's strength and his role.
Finding a gap in the market and creating value in people's lives are the results of his fortune.
Richard Branson, this poem is a gesture for your incredible empowerment! Needless to say, your life is in tune.

Tesla

A powerful organization with a vision that cannot be surpassed,
Committed to electric, sparking the evolution.
Its mission is to accelerate the world's transition to sustainable energy.
Founded in 2003 by a group of engineers to drive electric.
Tesla is truly a universal choice, having its ticks.
Under Elon Musk, one of the greatest entrepreneurs of this generation,
Tesla manages to become a household name, an astonishing creation.
Bringing electric cars to the mass market was its compelling goal.
Indeed, it has triumphed beyond expectations, leading a remarkable role.
Tesla is resilient and able to move along with the current issues in the automotive industry.
Conventional is so yesterday; unconventional is the new language surrounding Tesla.
Innovation is the key for the organization to be relevant and to develop cutting-edge electric cars.
A strong belief in addressing the problem from its roots.
Imagination of Tesla is beyond what one can perceive in the realm.
Think like owners is the principle from which its success truly stems.
Rather than making analogies, the root factors to understanding problems are imperative.
Becoming every customer's first choice, a brand to never be forgotten is the ultimate desire.
Forging ahead in unity to being a classic, transmitting hope, and igniting passion filled with fire.

Amazon

Obsessed over customers' priorities,
Amazon has truly stood its ground.
Working backwards and keeping customers' trust is the way it rolls,
Embedding principles that truly represent the organization.
Expect and require invention; simplify, be externally aware and perched for ideas, and look forward for that creation.
Drawing forth what lies within people and raising the performance bar, developing leaders and coaching others is primarily its role.
Aim for the relentlessly high standards that can surpass reality.
Operate at all levels, stay connected to the details, audit frequently, and be sceptical when metrics and anecdote differ.
Benchmark yourself against the best and create a development stir.
Focusing on the results and winning over setbacks is its constant aim.
Aim higher with the available resources.
American entrepreneur Jeff Bezos is one of the richest people in the world.
Amazon has truly created value in everyone's lives, a whirlpool of twirl.
The vision is to be the earth's most customer-centric company,
To build a place where people can find and discover online.
Amazon will continue to serve people and create value focusing on the present time.

Emirates Airline

One of the world's largest airlines.
Without a skip of its heartbeat, it has rapidly grown in its partnerships and expanded its role,
Existing to deliver the world's best in-flight experience.
Borders are so yesterday; it triumphs over any fence.
Ensuring aviation industry safety, leading and sustainable.
Emirates has a deep soul.
With a network of over 150 destinations across six continents, it is expanding across the world dramatically.
Evolving and moving along with time is the key.
Delivering higher standards of service quality to support business in the air transport industry is its main goal.
Recruiting numerous nationalities, incorporating unity in diversity, and channelling its energy are indeed its main roles.
Launched in the year 1985, one of the biggest fleets of Airbus 380 and Boeing 777,
It still continues to mesmerize people, flying over 25,000 feet, portraying its logo.
Management and leadership are imperative for an organization to succeed.
Integrity and honesty are required for them to feed.
Established in the year 1985, it truly captivates your attention with its breathtaking advertisements.
Its global reach to make someone's day without any bent.
The chairman of the airline, Ahmed Bin Saeed Al Makhtoom, is a true visionary, leading Emirates to be a magnanimous brand.
Taking your breath away is its new giant 777 fleet, astounding.
Emirates Airline, winning over hearts, surpassing boundaries, connecting to people's hearts, in alignment and sync.

Maserati

A symbol of motoring excellence that once could not be fathomed.
Its vision, enthusiasm, turned out to be the cornerstone.
Maserati had an impact on the world indeed, proving its credibility has immensely grown,
Forging its character and personality, bringing glorious achievements along the road.
Creating evolution with unique, elegant cars yet sporty, distinctive lines.
Stunningly beautiful, getting a sparkle, indeed aligned.
The trident, the symbol of myth, used on all racing cars remained constant across the brand and its style.
An exceptional brand that has touched millions of hearts is unconventional.
The greatest road is the one that lies ahead of you.
Maserati prides himself on his company's long and glorious heritage.
Little did the Maserati brothers know its comprehension and its scope,
Started in the heart of Bologna and cascading its impact across the globe.
Showering with unprecedented praise without a skip of doubt deserves a robe.
Working tirelessly in 1926 to design a miracle.
Maserati outshines in 1993; then the unthinkable happened.
Ferrari and Maserati joined forces,
Outshining their historic rivalry.
The pioneering innovation is beyond the comprehension of our minds.
Get closer to Maserati and enjoy its brilliance.
A brand that is breathtaking, surpassing any fence.

Disney

Diversified worldwide entertainment company with operations in four business segments across the globe.
Winning millions of hearts, indeed, it has truly maintained its credibility for generations.
Media networks, studio entertainment, parks, experiences, consumer products, direct-to-consumer, and international truly capture its segments.
Little did the world know that Disney's experimentation with the camera would lead to an animation invention.
Creating one of the best motion pictures across the world, winning twenty-two Academy Awards, and creating the cartoon character Mickey Mouse, it indeed was legendary.
Theme parks Disneyland in California and Walt Disney World in Florida are truly mesmerizing.
Four success principles of Walt Disney can bring forth the brightest that lies within you.
Believe in the big thing all the way, implicitly and unquestionably.
Dare when you are curious; you will find lots of things to do.
Study the project not at its surface but everything about it; that is the way to its success and its queue.
A creator and innovator, his flair for art and creativity was his greatest trait.
Keeping up with technology and carrying out his mission, forging ahead,
A true legend to be remembered without a skip of a beat.
A charismatic character who served as an inspiration to all his employees.
Disney, an American conglomerate headquartered in Burbank, California, still exists to serve its purpose,
Taking us to a dream world without any inhibitions, establishing a trust.
Disney will never forget to put a smile on our faces.
An organization that truly inspires humans to live without creating borders or eliminating traces.

BMW

Created in 1917 from the Munich firm Rapp Motorenwerke,
The company incorporated before being refounded as BMW AG in 1922.
Successor of Bayerische AG, founded in 1916, indeed holds its credibility today.
Inspired by the core principles taking leaders from success to success,
Accepting no compromises, setting exact standards, and then exceeding them.
Follow your instincts; make decisions an extension of your instincts.
Dare to innovate; pioneer technologies that make change happen.
Focus on the bigger picture, knowing when to take the back seat.
Assemble a strong team, drawing forth the potential and ensuring that it stands on its feet.
Exercise the privileges that come with the position.
Humility is indeed the foundation.
Move in collaboration with time, evolving and growing and adapting the future.
Uncompromisingly focus on the premium; BMW group automobiles and motorcycles inspire people around the world.
Sheer driving pleasure, sporty and dynamic performance combined with superb design and exclusive quality,
Winning millions of hearts as its exclusivity sets people free.
Being the centre of attention, it is indeed designed to take your breath away,
Forging ahead with vitality and shining with brilliance, emitting boundless rays.
An incredible legendary brand that refuses to be defeated.
Filled with the desire to bring forth innovation, standalone created.

Samsung

Committed to complying with the laws and regulations within the global code of conduct to all employees,
Building a trust within the global environment and trusting its employees to practise transparent corporate management,
Samsung has truly stood its ground of being committed without any inhibitions.
Bridging the gap, it shouts out loud that borders are so yesterday by bringing the customers together under one umbrella.
Competing strongly on fair grounds without being unethical is its primary goal.
It respects transparent accounting through transparent records.
Samsung is truly inspiring with its ethical determination without any odds.
Respecting political rights and political decisions of the company is imperative for it.
Segregating political powers, it does not use manpower facilities for political purposes.
Protecting and respecting intellectual property of the company and other people.
Samsung is committed to holding its head high.
Putting shareholders as its top priority without any question why.
Pursuing an eco-friendly environment and sustainability,
Puts customers' health and safety as its primary instrument, and that is the key.
It sincerely understands the responsibility of tax payments.
Provides equal opportunities for employees and treats them fairly according to their abilities and performances,
Samsung is going above and beyond, knocking down all fences.
Respects the social and cultural characteristics, and has cooperative management that is seemingly liberal.
Actively participates in disaster relief and volunteer work across the globe.
Samsung has truly stood its ground without any hesitations, earning a blanket robe.

J. P. Morgan and Chase

Born into a prominent New England family in 1837, J. P. Morgan
began his career in the New York financial industry in the late 1850s.
Cofounded the banking firm that became J. P. Morgan and Co. in
1871.
Establishing himself as the power player in the country's railroad
industry was the key,
Amassing immense wealth through the creation of such
corporations as US Steel.
Morgan led efforts to bail out the US Treasury; it seemed every
effort was on an incessant wheel.
Leaving behind a world-renowned art collection and a business, a
financial powerhouse into the twenty-first century.
An insatiable amount of growth, capturing countries across the
planet is synonymous to branches unshakable on a tree.
Father of J. P. Morgan helped investors and made his fortune.
J. P. Morgan has invariably stood its ground and been in tune.
Founded in the year 2000 in New York City,
It truly holds its credibility.
Exceptional client service has been its primary goal.
Focusing on the customer, it operates on the local level.
Building world-class franchises and investing for the long term to
serve its clients have truly expanded their horizon beyond what one
can fathom.
Setting highest standards of performance,
Demanding financial rigor and disciplined risk maintains a fortress
balance sheet.
Executing with both skill and urgency, it is always on its feet.
Hiring and retaining great diverse employees,
Maintaining an open entrepreneurial meritocracy for all,
Not compromising on integrity, facing facts, and having fortitude
Fosters an environment of respect, inclusiveness, humanity, and humility.
J. P. Morgan's approach is sincere and not on mute.
It helps strengthen the communities in which we live and work.

J. P. Morgan is disciplined at everything it does.
With great client relationships and great financial records, it is one of the few banks across the globe that deserves its due.
Merger of Chase Manhattan, the third-biggest banking company in the United States,
Acquiring J. P. Morgan & Co., one of the most storied banks across the globe,
Chase represents the firm's commercial banking and retail banking, while J. P. carries asset/wealth management and investment banking with an embroidered robe.
Its mission is to offer the best financial services in the world, focusing relentlessly on carrying out business principles, aspiring to be client-focused, creating indeed a twirl.
It aspires to be the best, execute superbly, and build a great team and a winning culture is its vision that is beyond.
A commitment to integrity, fairness, and responsibility are the embedded values.
Expression of being speechless, I am left with the completion of this immense gratitude,
As JPMorgan Chase indeed, without a doubt, has fortitude.

Bank of America

Bank of America, headquartered in Charlotte.
History dates to 1904, when Amadeo Peter Gianni opened the Bank of Italy in San Francisco.
Eventually developing into Bank of America and was for a time owned by Gianni's holding company.
One of the world's leading financial institutions, serving individual consumers and large corporations with banking, investing.
Bank of America, one of the big four major banks, continues to hold its accountability with a piece of string.
Deliver quality and reliability in client service is paramount.
Trust, belief, and transparency in all interactions.
Empowerment, embracing diversity and inclusions without any fractions.
Mission is to help lives by connecting clients and communities across the globe.
New slogan has captivated its attention: "Life is better when we are connected."
Concentrating on lives becoming financially stable without being hampered or being affected.
Responsibility, accountability for actions
Promoting potential to build a better future.
Delivering together, believing in the importance of treating each client and teammate as an individual and treating every moment as imperative.
Trusting the team, bringing unity in diversity, propelling work, creating a stir.
Leadership delivers for its clients and shareholders through a strategy of responsible growth and a culture of accountability.
Business strategies that are people-focused and thriving on building client relationships,
Focusing on environment, sustainability, and creating a better world.
Driving economic and social progress empowering women, creating a twirl.

Managing risks and providing a return to the clients and businesses are the intentions.
Delivering strong, consistent, high-quality results without any intervention—
A reason why Bank of America is one of the biggest around the existing realm.
Needless to say, it has been indomitable and unshakable from where it stems.

Wells Fargo

They are committed to being the best they can be—for each other, their customers, their communities, and their shareholders. They have the will and the drive to build a better world.
The reason they wake up in the morning is to help customers, succeed financially and to satisfy financial needs.
Wells Fargo is truly based on customer satisfaction without any greed.
Known for its classic stagecoach logo, it is the largest mortgage and auto lender in the United States.
Its expansion is beyond what one can fathom with unshakable gates.
Henry Wells and William Fargo founded Wells Fargo to serve the West.
Their enduring vision of helping customers succeed financially unites Wells Fargo.
Placing customers at the centre of everything it does,
Exceeding customer expectations, and building relationships that last a lifetime.
Striving to attract, develop, motivate, and retain the best team members without being subjected to any crime.
Committed to the highest standards of integrity, transparency, principled performance, doing the right thing, and holding accountability.
Valuing and promoting diversity and inclusion in all aspects of business and at all levels.
Success comes from inviting and incorporating diverse perspectives without any concealed motives.
Calling everyone as leaders, wanting everyone to lead themselves, lead the team, and lead the business.
In service to customers, communities, team members, and shareholders,
Uniting around a simple phrase.

Wells Fargo serves better a relationship with a trusted provider that
knows them well.
Wells Fargo continues to expand incessantly, without a single
moment of doubt or dwell.
Enduring principles will serve customers and help them each day.
Forging ahead, breaking the dawn with the shining ray.

Tuli Imperial Hotel

Step into the paradise; Tuli Imperial will surround you with beauty and paradise.
It is indeed a selection of unique people who undoubtedly are wise.
Ambience of the place is bewitching and fabulous.
A well-deserved holiday, truly mesmerizing are its surroundings.
Takes you on a luxury ride wrapped in red carpet wings.
Friendly and considerate towards every guest who boards,
Sending a spill down your spine.
Reminder of where history is lived and their ancestors have built upon.
A glance through the hotel will take your breath away.
Seemingly beyond what one can fathom is its comfort with the dawn of the morning ray.
Refreshing dip in the pool will make you a believer in a majestic world.
Gymnasium and health club will increase your energy levels,
Drawing forth the best among the people who felt at times dishevelled.
The definite place to go in town,
Creating a flutter in your chest.
A visionary hotel, ambitious and enriching,
Expanding on a magnanimous scale is its inherited destiny.
A strong belief in learning and growing is the foundation of becoming better than yesterday, Tuli Imperial discloses as its key.

Jumerah Group

A global icon of Arabian luxury that will seemingly take your breath away.
A land of architectural innovation.
A hotel that is embedded in creation.
Borders are so yesterday, and ideas can surpass limitations.
A hotel that's home to cutting-edge engineering, from a unique man-made beach and infinity pool terrace to the world's tallest atrium.
Exquisite dinning at Muntaha will fulfil your deepest desire for an extraordinary cuisine.
An evening that will create memories that are truly encapsulating.
Dining by Michelin-starred chefs.
A spectacular world-class spa.
An icon of the Dubai skyline, where history is lived.
Down to every last detail,
Burj Al Arab takes hotel design to a new level of modern luxury.
Sumptuous surroundings, unforgettable stays forever in our hearts.
A new beginning that will uncover numerous memories—indeed, a miraculous start.
Spectacular sea views filling each day with adventure.
Burj Al Arab encompasses glamour and a pure soul.
Fascinating every eye with its gravitas is its determined role.

Twitter

An American microblogging and social networking service.
Users post and interact with messages known as tweets.
Twitter, a unique platform to connect people on which they feed.
Tweets originally restricted to 140 characters exceeded its limit.
Limit doubled in 280 characters.
Based in San Francisco, more than twenty-five offices around the world,
Twitter has indeed created its landmark.
This organization has created quite an arc.
Its mission is the power to create and share information instantly,
Bringing people together; unity in diversity is the key.
Talented diverse employees work together worldwide.
Purpose for creating a Twitter account is to network online.
The membership advances, creating an era that will shine.
The first tweet posted by Jack Dorsey, the CEO, sent from space.
The original name—Status—perhaps seemed unappealing.
Short bursts of inconsequential information and chirps from birds hit the bullseye.
Inspired by Flickr, Dorsey initially called it "twttr" and later changed it back to Twitter without any questions or explanation.
Named after Larry Bird from the NBA'S Boston Celtics, Twitter's
Larry Bird logo had a slightly more intricate plumage.
Twitter, a symbolic representation based on a mountain bluebird.
Falling in love with social media more and more, a proper logo was introduced.
The little bird with a tuft of hair seemed infused.
Twitter bird summed up the objectives in a perfect way.
A brand that created a revolution on its own.
Surpassing boundaries, rock solid as the undaunted stone,
Twitter continues to go above and beyond where borders are so yesterday.
Throwing insatiable opportunities for people to explore and evolve without being swayed.

Talented and diverse employees work together across thirty-five offices worldwide,
Growing a business in a way that makes us proud.
Recognize that passion and personality matter.
Defend and respect the user's choice.
Twitter has its own independent voice.
Communicate fearlessly to build trust.
Reach every person on the planet across all borders.
Innovate through experimentation.
Seek diverse perspectives.
Ship it, be rigorous, and get it right.
Twitter's foundation is built on connecting humanity and not a fierce fight.
Simplify and make things easier for the exchange of words to progress.
Twitter focuses on interacting with harmony and not creating a mess.
Reaching every voice is its goal.
Twitter is indeed on a great mission and playing its unique role.
Refection in the mirror is paramount for the organization.
Twitter's foundation is based on immense creation.
People from across the globe comment on its everlasting expansion.
Twitter continues to surprise people and enrich them.
A rock-solid foundation built from which they stem.
Twitter will leave a legacy behind as it unfolds and grows.
Its incessant ability to foster and build relationships indeed flows.

Nike

Nike states, "It is our nature to innovate."
Nike is a company, a brand that simplifies and makes it easier for the consumer.
Evolving immediately and doing the right thing without an iota of doubt,
Nike's aim is to inspire people across different countries,
Mastering the fundamentals and refining its performance every day.
Innovation in the world has no value if not put into action.
Immense craftsmanship is required when ideas are executed, resulting in creation.
Making skilful decisions is key to its success.
Keenly aware of the customers' sophistication and treats them as key stakeholders.
To be honest and transparent and to promote diversity and sustainability,
Nike sees itself in perpetual motion, and that is indeed the key.
Nike encourages employees to be like a sponge, open to new ideas whatever their source,
Urging people to act like leaders in their field to achieve victory.
Nike's simplicity is attractive and spreading throughout the globe.
Their advertisements inspire ideas and make one ponder.
Eighty per cent are about the brand that has created value over the years.
A great athlete, running the marathon wearing Nike shoes, representing no fears.
A brand that makes you feel at ease.
Nike's existence is rock solid and will never cease.

Emirates NBD

Every day it makes its products simpler,
Providing solutions that will help them to fulfil financial aspirations.
Emirates NBD's commitment towards the nation with disabilities' support is incredible.
Supporting a world where barriers for people are so yesterday.
Embracing people across the globe with the ray of dawn,
Creating a friendly environment where the world comes to bank.
Initially formed as National Bank of Dubai in 1963,
NBD merged with Emirates Bank International in 2007,
Marking the group's outstanding achievements; Emirates NBD is the leading banking group in the Middle East,
The most trusted and reputed bank in the Middle East.
The bank that surpasses boundaries without any inhibitions,
Creating a collaborative environment by engaging employees through multiple channels and avenues.
Opinions are heard, and self-expression is encouraged.
Diversity is welcomed and embraced.
Care for its customers and employees is indeed not ephemeral.
Cultivating talent is a significant focus area at Emirates NBD.
Development and growth across all entities is its objective.
Its leadership and management development model captivate your attention.
The innovation model leaves you intrigued and inspired.
Emirates NBD brings the world together where everyone aspires to be hired.

Coke

The courage to shape a better future.
Collaboration to leverage collective genius.
Integrity to be real.
Accountability to step up.
Passion committed in heart and mind.
Diversity as inclusive as its brands.
Quality is in the brand.
Moving swiftly with the changing times.
Refresh the world in mind, body, and spirit.
Inspiring moments of happiness and through the brand and actions,
Creating value, and making a difference is Coke's mission.
Inspiring each other to be the best where a great place can be provided to work.
Offering the world a portfolio of drink brands that anticipate and satisfy people's desires and needs.
Coke breathes and emphasizes integrity,
Nurturing a winning network of partners and building mutual loyalty.
Being a responsible global citizen that makes a difference by helping to build and support sustainable communities,
Maximizing long-term return to shareholders, while being mindful of its overall responsibilities,
Being a highly effective, lean, and fast-moving organization across the globe.
Coke, running since history, carries a progressive robe
to build.

Oracle

A corporation in 1977 cofounded by Larry Ellison.
Inspired by a 1970 paper written by Edgar F. Codd on relational database management.
A relational model of data for large, shared databanks.
Based in Redwood Shores, California, it has truly stood its ground,
Specializing in developing and marketing database software and technology.
Values embedded symbolize integrity, demonstrating honesty and sound ethical behaviour in all business transactions.
Treating employees with respect and dignity.
Working together as a team with collective interests,
Sharing information effectively with one another.
Need for confidentiality regarding certain information.
Applying creative approaches to problem-solving, constantly working towards innovation.
Treating customer satisfaction as a top priority,
Make excellence and quality a part of day-to-day work processes.
Complying with all laws, regulations, and Oracle policies that govern.
Employees observe the standards that have been established by Oracle and act ethically in their approaches to business decisions.
Core values are imperative and need to be communicated.
Oracle, where customer satisfaction is at the top of the list to be initiated.
An incessant need for consistency has been an ongoing role.
Moving ahead steadily, as if in a marathon, Oracle refuses to subtract its role.

Microsoft

Founded by Bill Gates and Paul Allen to develop and sell basic interpreters.
Rose to develop the personal operating system followed by Microsoft Windows.
A vision is for every home to have a computer.
Windows was written from scratch by MS.
Developed its leadership principles in partnership with the NeuroLeadership Institute in 2016.
Creating clarity, moving team in the same direction, is what Microsoft is keen on.
Habits serve to turn somewhat abstract concepts into concrete behaviours.
Microsoft leadership principles are creating value every day.
Drive innovation that people love with the dawn of day.
Be without boundaries in seeking solutions.
Tenaciously pursue the right outcomes,
Generating energy not only in their teams but across the company.
Developing deeply shared understanding within teams and defining a course of action are the keys.
Internal and external noise; synthesize the message from it.
Define a course of action, and get everyone on the same page;
Microsoft is unrestricted and on the same page,
Inspiring optimism, creativity, and shared commitment,
Making an everyday environment and creating value.
Changing the culture at Microsoft doesn't depend on the leader.
It depends on everyone, who must dedicate themselves to making work better every day.
Microsoft continues to grow incessantly with immense rays,
Developing, manufacturing, licensing, supporting, and selling computer software, consumer electronics, and the personal computers Microsoft is best known for.
It truly encompasses its mission to empower each and every person and every organization on the planet to achieve more.

Being diversified in its choices and learning about innovation as ideas can be vast in dimension are truly its values.
Drawing forth the limitless potential branded under "Your Potential, Our Passion" is the cue.
Strengthening and safeguarding the culture of business integrity is primarily its goal.
Applying the power of technology to ensure corporate responsibility, safeguarding human rights, and protecting our planet are its roles.
Microsoft is indeed an imperative organization; its legendary success has bypassed innumerable boundaries, by creating the outstanding Microsoft Office Suite.
Microsoft Office Suite has served as an instrument for its greater growth.
Generating an enormous amount of revenue, this software has indeed served its purpose; looking ahead,
Its perseverance is inevitable.
Without a skip of a heartbeat, it is surely an act that is creating abundant value in an individual's life.
The founders were attacked by the competitors who penetrated like hidden knives.
It has surely stood the test of time.
Microsoft's manifestation into reality was indomitable; although trolled by numerous others, it was never subjected to crime.

Toyota

Its history began in 1933, with the company being a division of
Toyoda Automatic.
Direction of loom works under the direction of the founder's son.
Automobile manufacturer best recognized for building reliable cars.
An outstanding record for offering reliability and durability.
Known for providing convenience, comfort, and safety to its customers.
Toyota Motor Corporation, a Japanese automobile manufacturer,
creating a stir.
Decades have passed since Toyota came into existence.
Impressive resale value without any restrictions or fence.
Honours the languages and spirit of the laws of every nation,
Undertaking open and fair business activities to be a good
corporate citizen of the world.
Respects the culture and customs of every nation and contributes to
economic and social development activities.
Dedicating the business to providing clean and safe products is the key.
It fosters a corporate culture that enhances both individual creativity
and the value of teamwork.
Honouring mutual trust and respect between labour and
management is indeed quite a perk.
Create and develop advanced technologies and provide
outstanding products and services.
Pursue growth through harmony with the global community via
innovative management.
Toyota's contribution is legendary across the globe.
Its standing is worth its presence.
Toyota touches every human's heart
Through its ability to be accessible to diverse people.
Toyota has truly created a mark for itself.
It will always be the consumer's home car.
Toyota is and always will be a rising star.

Audi

The modern era of Audi began in 1960 when acquired by Volkswagen. Relaunched the Audi brand with the 1965 introduction of the Audi F103 series.
Volkswagen merged Auto Union with NSU, creating the present-day form of the company.
Setting an example—being responsible and authentic, words matching its actions.
Treating people with appreciation and respect.
Faith in the capabilities of the employees.
Encouraging them to be responsible in their actions and decisions.
Providing them with the necessary freedom and standing with them whenever required.
Prioritize corporate and project goals over departmental and individual interests.
Making every effort to live the agreed-on project and process goals.
Success is built on the abilities of employees.
Support and encourage employees to personally develop their goals,
Taking time to offer challenging tasks and supporting them individually company-wide.
Thinking outside the box and encouraging employees to think in new directions.
It gives them the support they need.
Having the courage to take responsibility and acting with entrepreneurial spirit and integrity is their feed.
Getting mistakes out in the open,
Audi does not look for anyone to blame.
Recognizing mistakes early and using them to improve the company, indeed not a game.
The world and internationalization are its market.
Growth happens around the world, encouraging intercultural experiences and ways of thinking.
Audi will continue to win people's hearts and supremely excel in consistency, demonstrating the attributes of a king.

Walmart

An American discount store chain began in the 1950s,
Introducing its warehouse club chain, Sam's Club, in 1983.
By the second decade, the chain grew to 11,000 stores.
Commit to your business.
Believe in it more than anybody else.
Exceed at work; catch the passion like a fever.
Share profits with associates, and treat them as partners.
Performing beyond your wildest expectations is the goal.
Motivate partners by setting high goals, encouraging competition,
and then keeping score.
Walmart was founded to excel like a lion's roar.
Communicate everything you possibly can to your partners.
Appreciate everything the associates do for the business.
Celebrate success, loosen yourself, show enthusiasm, and have fun.
Listen to everyone around you.
The key to success is not getting swept away, and that is the cue.
Exceed your customers' expectations; that is Walmart's primary role.
Swim upstream; go the other way, and ignore the conventional
wisdom.
Control your expenses better than your competition.
Run an efficient operation, and be a part of the solution.
Commit wholeheartedly towards the expansion of Walmart.
Employees of Walmart, stand by.
Walmart has and will continue to deliver beyond what one can
fathom as they focus on why.

Boeing

Its origin dates to 1916, when the American timber merchant William E. Boeing founded Aero Products Company.
Developed a single-engine, two-seat plane.
Boeing has truly stood on its name,
Taking the high road by practising the highest ethical standards.
Honouring commitments, taking responsibility for actions,
Striving for first-time quality and continuous improvement in all to exceed standards of excellence.
Value human life and health, and above all, take action accordingly to maintain the safety of the workplace.
Value skills, strengths, and perspectives of the diverse team.
Foster a collaborative workplace that engages all employees in finding solutions for Boeing's customers.
A responsible partner, neighbour, and citizen to its diverse communities and customers.
Promotes the health and well-being of Boeing people without creating a stir.
By operating profitably and with integrity, it provides customers with the best value innovation.
Enables employees to work in a safe and ethical environment.
Conducts business lawfully and ethically, and helps to strengthen communities around the world.
Acting with integrity, consistency, and honesty is the primary goal.
Values culture and creates an atmosphere where everyone has an opportunity to contribute.
Primary importance is on safety without any sort of refuting.
Advances on its common business objectives,
Focusing on the cause and not getting distracted by the effect.
Trust and respect make up the foundation that Boeing is built on.
A larger-than-life company that continues to inspire the people for which it was born.

Volkswagen

A car company from Germany.
The "people's car" in German.
Headquarters in Wolfsburg is truly mesmerizing.
Started in the 1930s at the request of the country's leader.
Takes on responsibility for the environment and society.
Is honest and speaks up when something is wrong.
Breaking new ground,
Volkswagen's journey is truly unique where it is found.
Living diversity,
Proud of the work it does,
Keeping the word and having a moral compass defines Volkswagen.
Volkswagen makes affordable mobility for millions of people,
Shaping mobility for generations to come,
Providing answers to the challenges of today and tomorrow.
Its core product becomes even more emotional and offers a completely new driving experience.
Being part of the solution when it comes to climate and environmental protection.
Its cars can continue to be cornerstones of contemporary individual and affordable mobility in the future.
Excited customers lay the foundation and are indeed loyal.
Attracting and retaining employees at Volkswagen and attracting the best global talents.
A role for the environment, acting with safety and integrity,
Becoming more transparent and agile,
Volkswagen has indeed its unique style.
An excellent employer and a place everyone looks forward to.
A company that truly deserves to be the people's car.
The time has arrived for its due.

Citibank

Founded in 1812 as the Citibank of New York.
Later became First National City Bank of New York.
It has 2,649 branches in nineteen countries, including 723 branches in the United States.
Has been established for centuries; indeed it is fate.
Delivers results.
Leads change.
Acts as an owner.
Works as a partner.
Builds great teams.
Citibank is a place where customers, after joining, have a scream of joy.
Leaders create unique value for internal and external clients based on expertise and in-depth knowledge of the stakeholder environment.
Building a culture of meritocracy and transparency,
Celebrating excellence with courage.
A world filled with curiosity and eagerness to learn without any rage
Enables economic values and positive social impact for government and communities.
A platform built on unity is the key.
Citibank works collaboratively across the firm and encourages employees to get the best results.
Raises champions with a culture of high standards.
Accepts challenges along the way,
Ensures systematic growth while driving performance,
Creating a moral compass without any boundaries and defence,
A clear path towards sustainable results.
Citibank will continue to exist.
A fundamental transformation surpasses without any twists.

PepsiCo

An American food and beverage company, one of the largest in the world.
Available in more than two hundred countries, it has taken a twirl.
Headquartered in Harrison, New York, PepsiCo specializes in manufacturing, marketing, and distribution.
Formed in the year 1965 with the merger of Pepsi-Cola, it continues to dwell with the spirit of innovation,
Care for the customers, and the world it lives in.
PepsiCo is driven by the intense competitive spirit of the marketplace.
Directs the spirit towards solutions that benefit both the company and constituents in the race.
Speaks with trust and care at all times,
Being honest and transparent, with its communications thoroughly understood,
Respects others and succeeds in collaboration.
Sells products it can be proud of.
Going above and beyond sincere innovation.
Win with diversity and engagement,
Embracing people with diverse backgrounds, traits, and ways of thinking.
Diversity brings in new perspectives, and orthodox ways are shrinking.
Balances short-term and long-term decisions,
Maintaining growth which is consistent across the globe.
PepsiCo indeed believes in environmental sustainability,
Improved performance in production, innovation,
And approaches in water-process technologies.
Striving for honesty, fairness, and integrity.
Continually striving to improve all aspects of society and economics, creating a better tomorrow than today.
PepsiCo will continue to shine with its incessant efforts with the dawn of the day.

Facebook

A social networking service launched and
Founded by Mark Zuckerberg with his college classmates.
Little did they know how big it would become; can the invented be subjected to destiny or fate?
Membership limited to Harvard students and then gradually to other colleges around Boston.
As it evolved, people felt stunned.
Core values of Facebook will intrigue you.
Making bold decisions, indomitable in its strength, and not afraid of being wrong some of the time.
Focusing on the impact and being part of the solution are its ultimate goals.
Expectations beyond the boundaries.
Excels in finding the biggest problems is its employment role.
Moving fast enables employees to learn faster.
A culture-builder creates a stir.
A belief that an open world is a better world.
Informed people make better decisions and have great impact.
Facebook is the platform, allowing one to enact the drama of one's own life without an act.
Creating value across the globe.
Facebook truly encompasses its potential with a shining robe.

www.ingramcontent.com/pod-product-compliance
Ingram Content Group UK Ltd.
Pitfield, Milton Keynes, MK11 3LW, UK
UKHW041917190726
13854UKWH00003B/1299